CONTENTS

WHAT IS BRAVERY?

When Britain has been at war, or after a terrible disaster has taken place, stories are told of men and women who perform amazing acts of heroism. Sometimes, people risk or give up their own lives to save the lives of others. This is called going 'beyond the call of duty', because people do more than is expected of them.

Throughout history, governments have always decorated soldiers and sailors for brave deeds in the heat of battle. However, the decoration of civilians is a newer idea and it was not until the second half of the 19th century that medals were awarded for civilian bravery.

In 1866, the Albert Medal was created to honour those who had saved a life. The Edward medal originated in 1907 and recognised brave acts in mines, quarries and other industrial sites. In 1940, the George Cross was established to be given for gallantry and is the highest civilian award.

◀ The George Cross is awarded for 'acts of the greatest heroism or courage in circumstances of extreme danger'.

CIVILIAN BRAVERY IN THE WORLD WARS

Peter Hicks

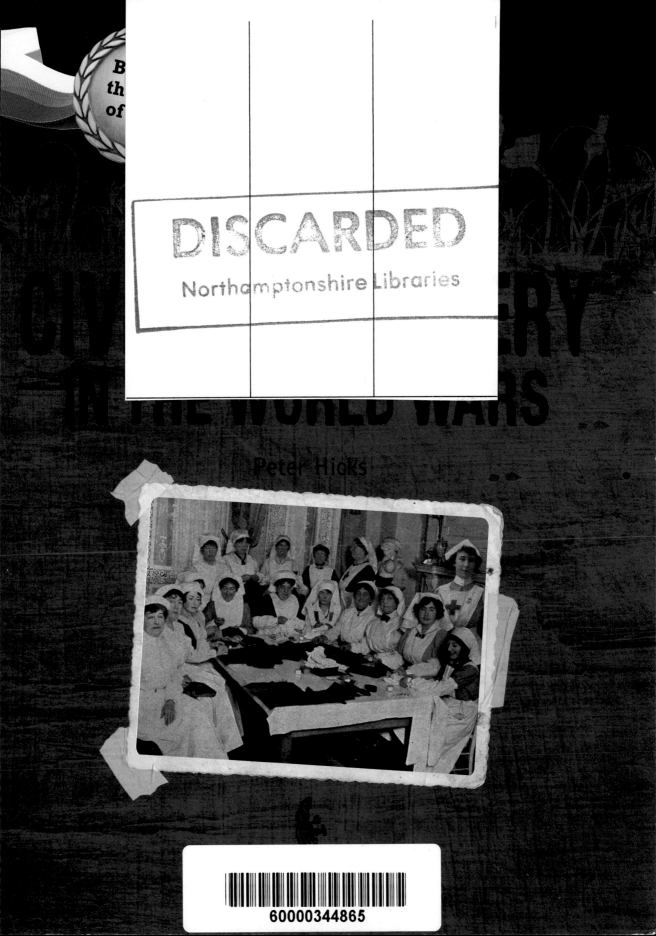

Published in paperback in 2015 by Wayland
Copyright © Wayland 2014

Wayland
338 Euston Road
London NW1 3BH

Wayland Australia
Level 17/207 Kent Street
Sydney, NSW 2000

Editor: Annabel Stones
Designer: Elaine Wilkinson
Author and main researcher: Peter Hicks
Researchers: Laura Simpson and Edward Field
at The National Archives

The National Archives looks after the UK government's historical documents. It holds records dating back nearly 1,000 years from the time of William the Conqueror's Domesday Book to the present day. All sorts of documents are stored there, including letters, photographs, maps and posters. They include great Kings and Queens, famous rebels like Guy Fawkes and the strange and unusual – such as reports of UFOs and even a mummified rat!

Material reproduced courtesy of The National Archives, London, England.
www.nationalarchives.gov.uk

Catalogue references and picture acknowledgements (Images from The National Archives unless otherwise stated): Cover (top left): MUN 5/297 HM Explosives Factory Gretna Dumfries (3) 1918; Cover (bottom left) & p.26: PRO 50/59 (106) Air raid precautions at Public Record Office, Chancery Lane; Cover (centre, medal): © Crown copyright 2013; Cover (right) & p.7 (top): ZPER 34/148 Red Cross Workers 1916 1; p2 & p.11 (top): AIR 1/569/16/15/142 Aftermath of Hull air raid, 1915; p.5 (top): INF 3/0486 GC Book Brandon Ross man rescuing woman from debris Artist O'Connell; p.5 (bottom): ZPER 34/148 Reservists Call-Up Notice 1916–l; p.6, p.9 (top left) & p.22: Shutterstock; p.7 (bottom): RAIL 253/516 Christmas and New Year card from the Front 1915–1918-l; p.8: Peter Hicks; p.9 (top right): De Agostini/Getty Images; p.10: AIR 1/7/6/98 (28) Crashed Zeppelin 19 December 1918; p.11 (centre): AIR 1/569/16/15/142 Course of Zeppelin, 1915.; p.12: Peter Hicks; p.13 (top): WORK 69/8 Silvertown explosion, scene looking South East from top of Firemen's tower, 1917; p.13 (bottom): MUN 5/289 National Projectile Factory Hackney Marshes Shell Stacks 1916-l; p.14: IWM via Getty Images; p.15 (top left): EXT 1/315/ Pt2 Women Come And Help poster WWI-l; p.15 (top right): NATS 1/1307 Women on board a train 1917-l; p.16 & p.30 (top): HO 338/27 Fire service work on bomb damaged building, 1940–1945; p.17 (top): FO 898/527 St Pauls Cathedral London partly obscured by smoke of bombs during the Blitz 1940-l; p.17 (bottom): INF 3/477 GC Book A E Dolphin man attempting to rescue nurse – wall collapsing, Artist Terence Cuneo; p.18: INF 2/73 4 The New Incendiary Bomb; p.19 (top left): RAIL 421/71 (1) Rail disaster, Curzon street, Birmingham 1940; p.19 (top right): INF 13/236 (2) Auxiliary Fire Service; p.20: AIR 28/75 (1) Merchant Ship sinking; p.21 (top): INF 3/1524 Allied Shipping Merchant ship convoy; p.21 (bottom): ADM 137/3907 German surface raider Moewe 1916; p.23 (top): INF 3/268 Anti-rumour and careless talk Ports are often bombed when convoys are in because somebody talked; p.23 (bottom): HO 192/200 Air raid damage Norwich 1942; p.24: RAIL 421/70 (24) West Ham station 7 September 1940; p.25 (top): RAIL 421/70 (20) Plaistow station 7 September 1940; p.25 (bottom): RAIL 253/327 (13) Swindon works war work 1939–1945; p.27 (top): CAB 98/62 Captured V2 rocket loaded on train 1945; p.27 (bottom): HO 192/625 (4) First V2 strike Staveley Road, Chiswick 8-9 September 1944; p.28 (above): HW 1/1 Churchill request to be sent Enigma messages daily 27 September 1940; p.28 (below): AIR 37/1031 (39A) Tedder to Churchill, railway bombing casualties, 23 May 1944; p.29 (top left): INF 1/244 Winston Churchill; p.29 (top right): E 329/475 Great Seal of Henry VIII 1531 obverse; p.28 (bottom): 800px-A gloved pair of hands at The National Archives. Background images and other graphic elements courtesy of Shutterstock.

A cataloguing record for this title is available at the British Library.

ISBN 978 0 7502 8423 3

Dewey Number 940.3'161

Printed in China
10 9 8 7 6 5 4 3 2 1

Wayland is a division of Hachette Children's Books, an Hachette UK company
www.hachette.co.uk

▲ Special Constable Brandon Moss worked for over seven hours to rescue survivors in a bombed house during the Coventry Blitz in November 1940.

Those civilians who were awarded a bravery medal were not the only people who showed courage during the World Wars. It just means that these acts were witnessed. Countless other acts of bravery and kindness took place that were not seen or recognised.

'When conditions became critically dangerous he alone worked his way through a space he cleared and was responsible for the saving of the three persons alive.'

Taken from the report of Brandon Moss's George Cross award.

Civilians at War

Before World Wars I and II civilians were only really affected by a conflict if they lived near to the battlefield, or an army marched through where they lived. The World Wars changed this, because they were examples of total war – when everybody became involved. Men and women were conscripted or 'called up' by the government, were asked to work in more dangerous jobs and both sides targeted industrial towns and cities. Civilians were now in the front line.

▲ Reservists are 'called up' for the armed forces in 1916.

TRAPPED BEHIND ENEMY LINES

When World War I began in August 1914, medical services for the British Army were not well organised. They could not cope with the large number of casualties so voluntary organisations and charities stepped in. One of them was the St. John's Ambulance.

Name:
Esmee Sartorius

Date:
August–November 1914

Event: German invasion of Belgium

Location:
Belgian–Dutch border

Medal:
The Mons Star

On 14 August, Esmee Sartorius, a member with just three month's training, found herself in Brussels, the Belgian capital. All the nurses were on standby because a large battle was expected. Then it was announced that the Germans were just outside the city and all Allied nurses and wounded would be evacuated. However, Esmee and her friends decided to stay and help. On 16 August, the Germans marched into Brussels. Esmee's group was sent by the Belgian Red Cross to the city of Charleroi where they were to join up with other British nurses at a hospital.

When they arrived, the city was in ruins and the hospital was full of French wounded. It was very nerve-wracking when German soldiers suddenly swooped into the wards looking for deserters or checking that French soldiers were not escaping. Luckily Esmee spoke French, so the Germans thought she was Belgian.

When the hospital was emptied of patients, the British nurses decided to try to escape back to Britain through neutral Holland. Their Belgian friends gave them some money and German papers that would get them to Liège, about 25 kilometres from the border. They crowded into an ambulance and set off. The ambulance could only take them so far, but by train, tram and walking they reached Liège.

From there, Esmee found a vegetable cart to hide in going to market at Maastricht, a town in Holland, but at the frontier

▲ Many women helped the war effort by volunteering for organisations such as the Red Cross.

A SECOND THOUGHT
Why do you think Esmee decided to stay in Belgium when everyone else went back to England?

the driver would only risk taking three people. Esmee, her friend and a Belgian got out and tried crawling under the frontier barbed wire. A sentry saw them and threatened to shoot! However, when Esmee showed him their papers he was impressed with the German stamp. Later, they managed to bribe another sentry, and they crawled under the wire into Holland. Within a few days they were at Folkestone.

The Schlieffen Plan

Esmee was trapped by the German invasion of Belgium. The German war plan, known as the Schlieffen Plan, was designed to avoid fighting France and Russia at the same time. The plan was to defeat France quickly, by going through neutral Belgium, surrounding Paris and then turning east to take on Russia. However, the German Army was slowed down by the Allied forces and failed to reach Paris. Russia entered the war much quicker than expected and attacked Germany in the east.

▲ This official British Christmas card shows 'Tommy' going into battle with rifle and pipe!

THE LADY ON THE BLACK HORSE

Mrs Mabel Ann St. Clair Stobart, an active campaigner for women's rights and a suffragist, founded the Women's National Service League in 1914 to 'provide service at home or abroad'. She set up a hospital for the Belgian Red Cross, but it was overrun by the Germans!

Name:
Mabel Ann St. Clair Stobart

Date:
October–December 1915

Event:
The Great Retreat in Serbia

Location:
The Balkans

Medal:
The Orders of The White Eagle and St. Sava

In 1915, Mabel Ann was asked by the Serbian Relief Fund to run a hospital in Serbia. She and her nurses set up a chain of clinics to help the thousands of Serbs suffering from typhus, diphtheria, smallpox and tuberculosis.

▼ **The difficult mountains of Montenegro that Mabel Ann's party had to cross to reach safety in Albania.**

All went well until October, when German, Austro-Hungarian and Bulgarian troops invaded Serbia.

It was very one-sided: 300,000 fresh troops with artillery against the tired, ill and poorly equipped Serbs. There was only one thing to do: retreat south.

Mabel Ann joined the thousands of women, children and old men fleeing the invaders. They had to travel over mountains into Montenegro to the safety of Albania. She was in charge of a hospital column and given the rank of Major – a first for a woman – but she preferred the title 'Maika' (mother). The column consisted of doctors, nurses, drivers, orderlies, ox-wagons, horse-drawn wagons and motor ambulances. She led them on a pony for the whole 1,300-kilometre trek, so journalists called her 'the lady on the black horse'. To keep the column together she put the ox-carts at the front so the horses had to keep to their pace.

Through mountain passes, in freezing conditions they crept towards safety. The roads became so narrow they had to cut the four-wheeled carts in half and abandon the hospital equipment. They melted snow to get water and the animals had to eat dead beech leaves. The bedraggled column reached Albania on 20 December. It had taken 81 days. The Serbian government decorated Mabel Ann with the Orders of the White Eagle and St. Sava.

A SECOND THOUGHT

What would people at home reading the story of Mabel Ann in the newspapers think about her exploits?

▲ The assassination of Franz Ferdinand and his wife in Sarajevo, Bosnia, on 28 June 1914.

War Begins

In June 1914, Serbia was at the heart of the conflict that sparked off World War I. The assassination in Sarajevo of Archduke Franz Ferdinand, heir to the Austro-Hungarian throne, was blamed on the Serbs. The crisis that followed pulled in all the other major European powers – Russia, Germany, France and finally Great Britain. Serbia won some minor victories against the Austro-Hungarian Empire early in the war. But, it was only a matter of time before Austria-Hungary, with help from Germany and Bulgaria, would try to 'deal' with Serbia once and for all.

ATTACK FROM ABOVE

World War I was the first conflict where civilians were directly in danger. Towns and cities experienced bombing raids by Zeppelins – large airships – from January 1915 until August 1918. The first raid on 19-20 August targeted Great Yarmouth, Sheringham and King's Lynn leaving four dead and 16 injured.

Name:
P.C. Charles Smith

Date:
24 September 1916

Event:
Zeppelin Raid

Location:
Peldon, Essex

Medal: Police Merit Star

Date Awarded:
September 1916

As more raids took place, the Royal Flying Corps and anti-aircraft batteries tried to defend big cities like London. However, the great height the Zeppelins achieved meant they often got through to drop their bombs.

On the night of 23–24 September 1916, Zeppelin L33 took part in a raid on the East End of London. Having dropped nearly three tons of bombs – killing six people

– the commander, Lois Bocker, turned the airship for home but was hit by an anti-aircraft shell. Losing height, the L33 limped across Essex but was attacked again by a squadron of night fighters. Bocker crash-landed the 197-metre airship

▼ Commander Lois Bocker destroyed his crashed L33 Zeppelin so it could not be of use to the British authorities.

Bombing Raids

Because of their high altitude, Zeppelin bombing accuracy was poor. As a result, the Germans began to send heavy 'Gotha' bombers over from Belgium to make more accurate raids on Britain. Starting in May 1917 they flew 22 raids over the south-east of England, dropping nearly 200,000 bombs and killing over 300 people. Civilian morale was affected, but these air raids did not seriously disrupt the war effort.

▲ Houses destroyed after a Zeppelin raid on Hull, 6–7 June 1915.

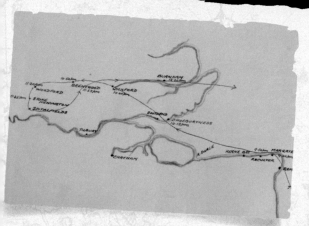

▲ This map show the route that many Zeppelins took when they attacked London and the Thames Estuary.

at Little Wigborough, just south of Colchester. He gathered his crew of 21 men and ordered them to set fire to the Zeppelin. They then marched off.

Special Constable Edgar Nichols met them on his bike and asked them if they had seen a Zeppelin crash. Bocker (in perfect English) asked: 'How many miles to Colchester?' Nichols answered: 'About six.' Nichols followed them at a distance until they reached the Post Office at the village of Peldon. Here they met P.C. Charles Smith who took charge.

Unarmed and faced with 22 enemy fliers, he calmly rounded them up and informed them they were under arrest and in his custody until they were handed over to the military.

Bocker asked to use the telephone but P.C. Smith refused. With some special constables he led them off to the nearby army camp. Luckily, they were met on the way by a squad of soldiers. P.C. Smith was promoted to Sergeant and awarded the Merit Star for 'coolness and judgement handing over to the Military Authorities the commander and crew of a Zeppelin'. From then on he was known to everyone as 'Zepp'!

A SECOND THOUGHT

He did not show it, but why do you think P.C. Smith was nervous when he faced the 22 German fliers?

AN AWFUL SPLENDOUR

Some of the most important items that Britain produced for the war effort were artillery shells. Their production required high explosives and one factory in Silvertown, in the East End of London, purified TNT – a very dangerous procedure.

Silvertown produced on average nine tons of TNT every week. Crude TNT was put into a giant cauldron, or melt-pot, as part of the process. On Friday 19 January 1917 at around 6.30 pm a fire broke out in the melt-pot room and quickly spread. The day-shift workers had just left the factory so there were only about 40 people on-site. Some of the men, including Dr Andrea Angel, the factory's chemist, and worker George Wenborne tried to bring the fire under control. Nearby, in the factory's railway sidings, were 50 tons of

▼ **Plaque remembering PC Greenoff in Postman's Park, City of London.**

P·C·EDWARD GEORGE BROWN GREENOFF

METROPOLITAN POLICE

MANY LIVES WERE SAVED BY HIS DEVOTION TO DUTY AT THE TERRIBLE EXPLOSION AT SILVERTOWN · 19·JAN·1917·

TNT packed into wagons ready to be taken away. P.C. Edward Greenoff saw the flames and rushed to warn members of staff to evacuate the factory area immediately.

At 6.52 pm the fire ignited the wagons of TNT causing a massive explosion that destroyed the factory and engulfed the surrounding area in a horrific inferno. A fireball lit up the neighbourhood, as a local journalist wrote: 'in an awful splendour. A fiery glow...over the dark and miserable January evening.' Red-hot lumps of metal and rubble were thrown through the air, causing more fires that raged out of control.

Very soon, large numbers of firemen, soldiers, police, nurses, doctors and ambulances flooded into Silvertown from all over London. Firemen struggled to tame the fire and it was not until Sunday afternoon that the fires were finally put out.

Dr Angel and George Wenborne were both killed in the blast and P.C. Greenoff suffered terrible head injuries. He died in hospital nine days later. They could have saved themselves, but they stayed to try to prevent more people being hurt. The disaster killed 73 people and injured over 600; 900 houses were destroyed and damaged, leaving thousands of people homeless.

▲ A scene of total devastation at Silvertown after the explosion in January 1917. Whole streets were destroyed.

A SECOND THOUGHT

The government opened the TNT factory in a crowded part of East London. Why did they take such a risk?

Increasing Production

There had been a scandal in March 1915 after the British Army ran out of shells during the battle of Neuve Chapelle. The government responded by building new factories to increase production of shells and explosives, such as cordite and TNT. The Silvertown factory had previously made caustic soda but was opened as an explosives factory in September 1915. Sadly, the Silvertown disaster was not an exception, and serious explosions took place at other munitions factories in Faversham (1916) and Chilwell (1918) causing great loss of life.

▲ The guns of the British Army and Navy had a greedy need for shells.

LEGION D'HONNEUR

The First Aid Nursing Yeomanry (FANY) was set up in 1907, with the idea that women horse riders would take wounded soldiers from the battlefield to the dressing station. They thought a single rider was faster than a horse-drawn ambulance. When World War I broke out, many women volunteered but drove motor ambulances not horses!

Name:
Henrietta Fraser

Date: July 1918

Event:
2nd Battle of the Marne

Location:
Near Rheims, France

Medals:
The Croix de Guerre and Légion d'Honneur

Although the British Army was poorly prepared for the thousands of wounded at the start of the war, it rejected the FANY's offer of help. Some people in the War Office thought it 'not proper' for women to go to war. Instead, the FANY opened hospitals and casualty-clearing stations, and drove ambulances for the Belgian and French Armies.

Henrietta Fraser was a cousin of the British Expeditionary Force's Commander-in-Chief, Douglas Haig, and she desperately wanted to do something for the war effort. After joining the FANY, she found herself driving with the French Army near the River Marne in 1918. In July, the French launched an offensive against the Germans at Rheims. The casualties were high and

▼ **FANY ambulance drivers wrapped up in their fur coats.**

◀ While working-class women tended to apply for factory work (wages were relatively high), middle and upper class women tended to volunteer for nursing.

▲ A train leaving Cardiff with nurses bound for hospitals in France.

the job difficult. Henrietta's work included evacuating hospitals, taking the wounded to safe areas and driving along roads crowded with refugees. German planes bombed the French positions at night, so the drivers got very little sleep. They longed for bad weather to ground the planes.

One day, Henrietta was driving her ambulance full of wounded to a hospital, when it was hit by a massive explosion. The orderly next to her was killed instantly and Henrietta was severely wounded. Barely conscious, she crawled out of the wrecked ambulance and onto the ground. She knew the hospital was nearby and she began to crawl the 200 metres to get help for her patients. She reached the hospital and told the orderlies what had happened, but refused any treatment herself until her wounded had been taken care of. The French government were so impressed by her courage that they awarded her the Croix de Guerre and the coveted Légion d'Honneur.

Women and War

Women were keen to help the country as soon as war broke out in 1914, but it was not easy. When Dr Elsie Inglis tried to set up an ambulance unit in Belgium, a War Office official told her: 'My good lady, go home and sit still'. This attitude made women even more determined to help and by 1918 some 18,000 women were working for the military. The Voluntary Aid Detachment (VAD) also worked in hospitals, drove ambulances and provided catering both in Britain and overseas.

A SECOND THOUGHT
Why do you think women wanted to get involved and help the country when war broke out?

BLITZ!
. . . .

On Saturday 7 September 1940, the Luftwaffe – the German air force – stopped attacking RAF fighter stations and began to bomb London. The city was easy to find by following the River Thames. The London docks, through which most of Britain's essential supplies moved, was an important target.

Name:
Alfred Dolphin

Date:
7 September 1940

Event: The Blitz

Location:
New Cross, South London

Medal: George Cross

Date Awarded:
17 January 1941

▲ **Because so many working-class houses were packed close to factories and docks, thousands of homes were destroyed during the Blitz.**

On the evening of 7 September, the South East Hospital was badly bombed. The hospital kitchen in Ward Block 1 took a direct hit, killing four nurses on the ground floor, and injuring the night sister and some of the patients in a nearby ward. A nurse who was upstairs fell through the collapsed floor into a passage below. She was badly hurt, but still alive and trapped under piles of rubble.

One of the hospital porters, Alfred Dolphin, saw what had happened and rushed in with a group of workers to help free her. They started removing the debris by hand, but then heard a sudden crack and a wall started to collapse onto the group. They had time to get away before it fell, but Alfred Dolphin stayed where he was. He threw himself on top of the nurse to shield her from the falling masonry.

When the dust had settled the rescuers went back to find the injured pair. Alfred Dolphin was found dead, lying across the nurse with his head towards the wall that killed him.

Industrial Targets

The Luftwaffe's aim in the Blitz was to bomb Britain's industrial centres so badly that it would be impossible to continue fighting the war. Factories, railways, bridges, power stations, naval bases and docks were ruthlessly targeted. On 7 September, the first wave of bombers hit the docklands in the afternoon and they were soon ablaze. That evening, a second wave flew in guided by the flames. It was during this wave that the hospital was hit.

▲ The dome of St. Paul's Cathedral, London, in the smoke and fire of an air raid.

The nurse was found to be alive though critically injured. Alfred Dolphin, a married man, who had worked at the hospital for 20 years, had performed the ultimate act of courage.

Four months after his death he was posthumously awarded the George Cross. In his citation it said: 'There is no doubt that Dolphin, although aware the wall was going to collapse, deliberately remained where he was and threw himself in an endeavour (effort) to save her. This he succeeded doing at the cost of his own life.' Alfred's action is known as self-sacrifice.

A SECOND THOUGHT
What qualities did Alfred display during the air raid?

▼ Alfred Dolphin shields the injured nurse as the wall collapses...

FIREFIGHTER

As well as high-explosive bombs, the Luftwaffe also dropped incendiary bombs. These stick-like bombs were dropped from planes in batches of 72 and fell into gutters, drainpipes and chimneys. After a while they would flare-up and set fire to anything that was nearby. It was because of these that so many British homes were damaged.

Name:
Harry Errington

Date:
17 September 1940

Event: The Blitz

Location: Central London

Medal: George Cross

Date Awarded:
8 August 1941

Harry Errington was a master cutter for a tailor in London's Savile Row, where the best suits are made. When war broke out, he volunteered for the Auxiliary Fire Service (AFS), which trained men to be firefighters in their spare time. After a day making suits, Harry would put in a shift as a firefighter.

When the Blitz began in September 1940, there were not enough firemen to cope with the terrible fires that broke out. Harry found himself spending more time holding a hosepipe than cutting material.

THE NEW INCENDIARY BOMB IS HEAVIER than the older bomb and penetrates deeper

Search all floors including basement

▶ **This poster warns civilians to beware of incendiary bombs.**

During the night of 17 September, he and two friends were sheltering in the basement of the local AFS building in central London when it took a direct hit from a bomb.

Twenty people were immediately killed, including six firemen. Harry was thrown across the room, receiving heavy knocks and bruising. He picked himself up and was just about to leave when he heard groaning. Looking over, he saw one of his friends was pinned down by fallen masonry. The fire in the building was spreading quickly.

Covering himself with a blanket for protection against the heat, he dug out his injured comrade, badly burning his hands in the process.

▲ The charred remains of a Birmingham textile factory.

He pulled his friend to safety and left him in a courtyard outside. He then rushed back down for the second time. Another man was pinned under a large radiator, but Harry quickly freed him and carried him up to the street. Despite being badly burned his comrades both survived and by December 1940 all three were back fighting fires.

Harry was personally presented with his George Cross by King George VI at Buckingham Palace on 21 October 1941.

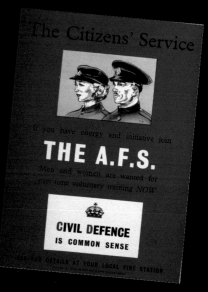

▲ Auxiliary Fire Service recruitment poster.

Fighting Fires

The AFS set up their own fire stations in schools, halls and garages. Their equipment was basic and often cast-offs from local fire brigades, it sometimes even had to be towed by taxis! It was difficult for the AFS to work with local firemen as their equipment didn't match or work together. As volunteers, the AFS were unpaid but still showed great commitment to their task. London was bombed for 57 consecutive nights and their contribution to the defence of the capital was immense.

A SECOND THOUGHT

What were the particular difficulties of being a fireman in your spare time?

SHARK-INFESTED WATERS!

The fact that Britain is an island certainly prevented an invasion in 1940. However, it also meant that it relied on imports to feed the population and keep factories producing arms. The Germans knew this and tried to sink as many supply ships as possible.

Name: David Hay

Date: 29 January 1941

Event: Battle of the Atlantic

Location: Off the coast of West Africa

Medal: Albert Medal

Date Awarded: 8 July 1941

On 14 January 1941 the SS *Eurylochus* left the port of Liverpool bound for Takoradi in Ghana. In her cargo hold were 16 heavy bombers (planes). The ship was part of Convoy OB 274, consisting of 49 merchant ships protected by two Royal Navy destroyers.

David Hay, a young cadet, was part of the crew. He had joined the Merchant Navy without telling his family. By 29 January SS *Eurylochus* was being shadowed by the German surface raider *Kormoran*. Without warning, *Kormoran* opened fire and soon SS *Eurylochus* was hit and on fire. She fired four shells in return, but was badly damaged and could not continue fighting.

When the ship's Master gave the order to abandon ship, David helped the crew to launch two life rafts under thick machine-gun fire from *Kormoran*. The German ship then fired a torpedo that sank SS *Eurylochus* and David and his comrades leapt into the sea and swam for the rafts. In the confusion, one of the rafts overturned. Most of the men reached the other raft, which became overcrowded. Suddenly, a group of sharks began circling nearby, their fins clearly visible in the water.

◄ A merchant ship sinks in the English Channel. Note the oil slick which was a danger for sailors swimming for survival.

David noticed the wireless operator, Colley, struggling in the water. He dived into the sea and swam to his aid. He had just got hold of him when a shark lunged towards them tearing David's clothes. Frantically kicking and twisting, David pulled Colley towards the raft as the shark attacked again. Just in time the pair were pulled from the sea by men on the raft! After 18 hours in rough seas, the raft was rescued by a Spanish ship.

▲ The Merchant Convoys were Britain's life-line during the war.

A SECOND THOUGHT

Why do you think David did not tell his family he was joining the Merchant Navy?

In Disguise

Kormoran was an auxiliary cruiser. It looked like a normal merchant ship, but this was just a disguise. In fact, it was a well-armed warship, carrying cannons, anti-aircraft guns, machine-guns and torpedoes. Her job was to sail the Atlantic and Indian Oceans looking for Allied supply ships, then sinking them. *Kormoran* had various false names and flags to baffle the enemy, such as the 'Saito Maru', a Japanese freighter, and the 'Straat Malakka', a Dutch merchantman.

▲ German surface raiders disguised as merchant ships were used in both World Wars.

HULL HAD NO PEACE

Kingston-upon-Hull on the east coast of Britain was the city worst affected by bombing during the war. Almost all of its housing was damaged, nearly 3,000 homes had to be demolished and 152,000 people were left homeless. Nearly 1,200 inhabitants were killed and 3,000 injured.

Name:
P.C. John Dobson

Date: 1941

Event:
The Hull Blitz

Location:
Kingston-upon-Hull

Medal:
The British Empire Medal

Date Awarded:
19 May 1942

It seems Hull was an easy target with its identifiable rivers – the Humber and Hull – and docks. Some believe the Germans thought the docks provided supplies for the convoys to the Soviet Union and were determined to disrupt them.

During a heavy raid in 1941, P.C. John Dobson of the London and North East Railway Police was on duty. He was trying to put out a number of incendiary bombs that had flared up in the railway goods yards by the docks. Suddenly, a bomb exploded close by and the blast knocked him into a building, which began to collapse.

Dobson found himself buried up to his shoulders in debris. Two other men were

also trapped and to make matters worse, the offices attached to the building were on fire and on the verge of collapsing. Dobson freed himself quickly and then dug out the other two men, but he was badly concussed and shaken up. Soon after, another bomb exploded near him and he saw the blast blow a fireman into a burning building. Despite his groggy condition he fought the heat and the flames and dragged the man out.

Dobson was awarded the British Empire Medal and his citation read: 'Dobson displayed courage and devotion to duty in difficult and dangerous circumstances.' He received it personally from King George VI.

Hull's raids were intense. On the night of 18–19 May 1942, 168 tonnes of bombs were dropped on the city, including one

Targeting the Ports

The Luftwaffe deliberately targeted ports in an attempt to disrupt industrial production and lower civilian morale. Ports tended to be densely populated with housing close by, so civilian casualties were high. London imported at least a third of Britain's supplies, but Liverpool, Newcastle, Glasgow, Belfast, Portsmouth, Plymouth, Bristol, Cardiff and Southampton suffered heavy raids too. Because many ships from America with essential supplies docked at Liverpool, it received many raids and at one point the port was only operating at 25 per cent capacity.

PORTS ARE OFTEN BOMBED WHEN CONVOYS ARE IN BECAUSE SOMEBODY TALKED

Never mention arrivals, sailings, cargoes or destinations to anybody.

▲ This poster warns people not to spread dangerous gossip in case spies were listening.

1,000kg bomb and another massive 1,800kg bomb that destroyed most of Scarborough Street near the Fish Dock. Nearly 300 incendiary bombs were dropped, causing widespread fires. The raid began just before midnight and when the all-clear siren went at 1.16 am, 50 people were dead and 58 seriously injured.

A SECOND THOUGHT
What do you think the phrase 'devotion to duty' means?

◄ Air raid damage in Norfolk. Homes all over Britain were destroyed by air raids.

"I would say that the town that suffered most was Kingston-upon-Hull...Hull had no peace."

Home Secretary, Herbert Morrison.

AMMUNITION TRAIN

In the summer of 1944, the roads and railways in Britain were very busy. Huge amounts of military equipment were transported to southern and eastern England. This activity was to prepare for an amphibious invasion of northwest Europe. Known as D-Day, it was planned for Tuesday 6 June.

Names:
Benjamin Gimbert and James Nightall

Date: 2 June 1944

Event:
Preparations for D-Day

Location: Soham Railway Station, Cambridgeshire

Medal: George Cross

Date Awarded: 25 July 1944

▲ Railway track peeled back by bomb damage.

Just after midnight on 2 June, an ammunition train of 51 trucks was being driven by Ben Gimbert and his fireman James Nightall to a USAF (US Air Force) base near Ipswich, Suffolk. Each wagon contained 44 500-pound bombs – a deadly cargo! As the train approached the station of Soham, Cambridgeshire, Ben noticed that the truck next to the engine was on fire. He told James and brought the train to a halt in the station. The truck was now burning furiously, so James immediately jumped down, uncoupled the wagon and re-joined Ben on the footplate. Ben's plan was to take the burning wagon clear of the station and town, where, if it did explode, it would do less damage.

The train had only travelled about 100 metres when the wagon exploded, killing James and seriously wounding Ben. The signalman on the opposite platform was critically injured

▲ Damage to the railways slowed the movement of essential equipment around the country.

and died the next day. Soham station was destroyed and the explosion made a huge crater 20 metres wide and 8 metres deep. Ben had been thrown high into the air and was taken to hospital where surgeons fought to save his life. During the first three days surgeons took 32 pieces of metal from his body. He spent seven weeks in hospital but went on to make a full recovery.

The two men's bravery averted a serious disaster. If they had not uncoupled the burning wagon, the whole ammunition train containing 450 tons of high explosive would have destroyed the town of Soham, killing hundreds of people.

A SECOND THOUGHT
What choices did Ben and James have to weigh up that night at Soham?

The Railways

The railways played an important role in the war and greatly contributed to victory. In 1939 they evacuated over a million children from cities in over 3,000 trains. They also helped to move huge numbers of troops, for example, when the 330,000 soldiers came back from Dunkirk in 1940. So important were the railways that the government took them over and controlled them centrally. Their finest moment came in 1944, when they took huge numbers of soldiers south to cross the Channel for the D-Day landings.

▲ The huge Great Western Railway works at Swindon made it a target for the Luftwaffe.

BEYOND HUMAN ENDURANCE

After the bombing raids of World War I, the Government was determined to improve the protection for civilians in the event of another war. Local authorities had to organise Air Raid Precautions (ARP), provide public air raid shelters, gas masks and take on people for work in civil defence and the emergency services.

Name: Albert Hemming

Date:
2 March 1945

Event:
2nd London Blitz

Location:
Bermondsey, South London

Medal:
George Cross

Date Awarded:
17 July 1945

▲ Air Raid Wardens at work protecting a public building from attack.

Albert Hemming was a Leader in the Civil Defence Rescue Service. This was a highly skilled, dangerous and important job. He had to assess bomb-damaged buildings and look for survivors. Albert was based in Bermondsey, in South London. Being near the docks, this was one of the worst hit areas of the city.

On 2 March 1945 after a V2 rocket attack, the Roman Catholic church and priest's house were badly damaged, as were 60 houses, 30 shops and flats and the nearby fire station. On arrival, Albert saw a scene of utter devastation and local witnesses told him people were trapped but they doubted anyone was alive. Floors had collapsed on top of each other and the debris and furniture was supporting the levels above. If this was disturbed the whole building would come down.

Albert heard a voice calling from the crypt and carefully dug in its direction. In the dark, with gas leaking from a broken pipe,

V Weapons

From the summer of 1944 till March 1945 there was a second Blitz. Nazi Germany launched their 'V' weapons on London and the south-east. 'V' stood for *Vergeltung*, meaning 'revenge'. The V1 was a jet-propelled flying bomb that carried a ton of high explosive. When it ran out of fuel it crashed and exploded. They killed over 6,000 civilians and injured over 18,000. The V2 was the world's first ballistic missile and it weighed 13 tons and crashed on its target at 3,000 mph.

▲ A V2 rocket. These weapons had a terrible effect on both cities and public morale.

the situation seemed hopeless. He saw a hand and methodically dug towards it. The survivor was pinned down by a large timber. If he moved it, they would both be killed. So Albert had to dig the debris out from below the man. After three hours of intense work, the survivor – Father Arbuthnot – was pulled from the wreckage.

It was an act of great heroism. Albert's George Cross citation read: 'Although…it appeared impossible to effect a rescue, Hemming refused to abandon the victim and with great gallantry and determination successfully accomplished a task seemingly beyond human endurance.'

▼ The scene of the first V2 rocket attack at Staveley Road, Chiswick, West London.

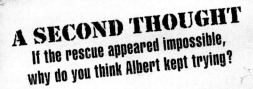

A SECOND THOUGHT
If the rescue appeared impossible, why do you think Albert kept trying?

RESEARCH AND RECORDS

In this book, you have learned about some exceptional acts of courage and bravery and the special people who carried them out. But where do these stories come from? How do we know Cadet David Hay leapt into shark-infested waters to save a comrade? Where is the evidence that Ben Gimbert and James Nightall saved Soham from destruction? Is there documentary proof that Harry Errington saved the lives of two other firefighters?

Historians studying the events of the past look for information and evidence to give them clues. Sometimes called the 'raw material' of history, this does not just exist in books that have been written before. After all, where did the information for these earlier books come from? Many historians start off in an archive, a place where important documents are stored.

TOP SECRET
and
PERSONAL.

37A

TOP SECRET

X

D/SAC/TS.100.

LOOSE MINUTE.

The Prime Minister.

Railway Bombi

You asked me in your
the score stands now. You will a
to get a really reliable estimate
us indicates that it is well with

2. According to Axis r
the score board reads as follows:-

Axis Reported
Killed.

6,062

These figures show that casu
are some 40% less than our e

3. Against these
already shows considerable
killed, including 285 of t
GERMANY to repair CREIL.
400 Germans celebrating H
Another valuable dividen
trains that have been bl

23rd May, 1944.

+ Final sentence,
German supply a

MOST SECRET.

10, Downing Street,
Whitehall.

September 27, 1940.

Dear C.

In confirmation of my telephone message, I have
been personally directed by the Prime Minister to
inform you that he wishes you to send him daily all
the ENIGMA messages.

These are to be sent in a locked box with a
clear notice stuck to it "THIS BOX IS ONLY TO BE
OPENED BY THE PRIME MINISTER IN PERSON".

After seeing the messages he will return them
to you.

Yours ever,

P.S. As there will be no check possible here,
would you please institute a check on receipt
of returned documents to see that you have
got them all back.

C.

◀ **Top secret documents sent to Winston Churchill during World War II. These can be studied at The National Archives.**

For example, if they were writing a book about Winston Churchill, they would visit an archive that contained his state papers, letters and notes. The biggest archive in Britain is The National Archives at Kew, in London.

◄ **Winston Churchill, Britain's war-time Prime Minister.**

▶ **The great seal of King Henry VIII attached to a document of 1531.**

The National Archives is the most important archive in the country and contains a huge range of official documents that make up the history of Britain. As well as important documents from the 20th century – especially the two World Wars – it contains written papers dating from the 11th century. If a historian wanted to learn more about Henry VIII's dissolution of the monasteries he or she would find whole files of records dating back between 1517 and 1560!

◄ **Some documents are so old and precious, researchers have to wear gloves to prevent damage.**

GLOSSARY

Air Raid Precautions (ARP) – An organisation set up to help protect civilians from air raids.

Allies – Countries that agree to help each other, especially in time of war.

Altitude – Height above sea level, or in a plane, the land.

Auxiliary Fire Service – During WW2, a volunteer fire service to support the local fire brigades.

BEF – The British Expeditionary Force, the British Army in France and Belgium 1914–18 & 1939–40.

Blitz – The bombing of British towns and cities 1940–45.

Cordite – A type of explosive that helps to propel shells and bullets.

Deserters – People who leave the armed forces without permission.

Diphtheria – A serious disease that causes problems with breathing and swallowing.

Evacuate – To move people away from a dangerous place.

FANY – The First Aid Nursing Yeomanry.

Gallantry – Showing courage in the face of danger.

Heir – The next in line to the throne.

Incendiary – A type of bomb that, after a delay, flared up causing fires.

Inferno – A large fire that is out of control.

Lenient – When a punishment is not severe.

Morale – The amount of confidence or enthusiasm a group of people have during testing or difficult times.

Neutral – When a country is independent and not aligned with another country.

Posthumously – A decoration awarded after a person's death.

Serbia – A country in the Balkans that was blamed for the assassination of Austria–Hungary's heir to the throne, Franz Ferdinand, in June 1914.

Reservists – People who are registered with the armed forces to be called up when needed. In World War I these were single men between the ages of 18 and 41.

Retreat – When an army moves away from the fighting to avoid defeat.

TNT – A powerful, yellow explosive, used in artillery shells.

Tommy – The nickname for British soldiers.

Tuberculosis – A serious disease of the lungs.

Typhoid – A serious infectious disease caused by dirty water or food.

VAD – Voluntary Aid Detachment, a voluntary organisation that provided nurses during World War I.

Western Allies – Britain, the United States and Canada. They attacked Nazi Germany from the West. The Soviet Union attacked from the East.

FURTHER INFORMATION

BOOKS

Children and World War 2 (History Snapshots)
by Sarah Ridley, Franklin Watts, 2011

One Child's War by Hugh Hanafi Hayes, CreateSpace, 2012

A Photographic View of World War One (Past in Pictures)
by Alex Woolf, Wayland, 2013

Road to War, My Story by Valerie Wilding, Scholastic, 2008

School Life (In the War) by Peter Hicks, Wayland, 2010

The First World War, 1914–18 by Pam Robson, Wayland, 2013

WEBSITES

www.nationalarchives.gov.uk/education
Website of The National Archives, with pages on both World Wars.

www.spartacus.schoolnet.co.uk/FWW.htm
A great online resource for information on the World Wars.

www.iwm.org.uk/history/the-british-home-front-during-the-second-world-war
A page from the Imperial War Museum on the British home front during World War II.

www.bbc.co.uk/schools/primaryhistory/world_war2/
Learn about children in World War II with this page from the BBC.

INDEX